Caucasian Kitchen - Cookbook

The best recipes from Georgian, Armenian and Azerbaijani cuisines

by

HANS MEYER

ISBN:9798722804365

The cuisine of the Caucasus is not just a tradition - but a whole culture!

The Caucasus is mountains that cannot be simply admired. Having visited once and talked with its people, you will never forget their hospitality, beauty of nature and wonderful air. The Caucasus is not just mountains, it is a whole culture of people, where they pay special attention to cooking, as well as ways of cooking and serving it. The long history of the cuisine of many people in the Caucasus is closely interconnected with their historical past. The cuisine of the Caucasus is usually the culinary delights of the inhabitants of the North Caucasus, as well as Transcaucasia. Different peoples have certain similarities in culinary preferences, but there are also some differences.

The cuisine of the Caucasus is characterized by the use of a large amount of various greens, as well as adding beauty to food, decoration, giving a taste that will not leave anyone indifferent. In Caucasian cuisine, most often they use asparagus, various types of spinach, celery, as well as most types of spices and always vinegar. High in the mountains, many herbs grow, which can be used for making herbs, and they can also prepare a certain dish from these herbs. Caucasian cuisine also has a special feature, these are various sauces, which are also made from herbs. The dishes are served along with the sauce, but it should be individual for each dish. This is done in order to emphasize the taste of meat, fish and vegetable dishes. In the Caucasus, the well-known "Adjika" is very popular, which is made from red pepper, some garlic, various coriander herbs and, of course, vinegar. Also very popular is the Chakhokhbili sauce, which, most importantly, has a large amount of onions.

Everyone knows that mainly Caucasian dishes are cooked on an open fire, on which they cook not only meat, called shashlik, but also fish along with vegetables.

The main place in the Caucasus is occupied by meat dishes. The dominant meats are lamb, veal, as well as beef and some types of poultry. One of the main items of Caucasian cuisine is barbecue. There are many ways to prepare it, but the main feature that unites all kinds of ways is its beautiful presentation. Basically, shish kebab is served with onions, chopped into rings, fried tomatoes, cucumbers, which can be different, both fresh and salted. Also in the cuisine of the Caucasus, meat is never turned into minced meat, and when chopping, a knife is usually used.

Absolutely any person who cares about their health needs to know those places on Earth where the traditions of healthy eating and the use of plant foods with maximum benefit are preserved. Caucasian cuisine includes fresh meat, vegetables, herbs, spices and red wine.

In the Caucasus, dishes made from fresh lamb, beef, veal and poultry are very popular. The people of the Caucasus are not used to passing meat through a meat grinder; they grind it by hand and just before cooking.

Shish kebab is the hallmark of Caucasian cuisine. They eat it hot. There must be chopped onions, fresh or baked tomatoes, eggplants, peppers and various herbs on the table. Eating fresh vegetables and herbs has a beneficial effect on the state of the body, enriching it with vitamins and fiber.

One of the most famous soups of Caucasian cuisine is a very thick, rich and delicious kharcho soup. It is made from beef, rice and walnuts. The latter contains a large amount of omega-acids, which prevent the development of cancer, the deposition of fat on the walls of blood vessels and help protect the human body from many diseases.

All dishes of Caucasian cuisine are abundantly decorated with various herbs. For example, dill, mint, basil, parsley. Sorrel, spinach, celery, etc. are also often used for cooking. Garlic, pomegranate juice and wine vinegar are added to almost all meat and fish dishes. Garlic helps the body fight disease-causing organisms, pomegranate juice contributes to better oxygenation of the blood, and wine vinegar contains a large amount of vitamins C and A, acids and minerals that improve digestive function.

In the Caucasus, red wine is always served with main dishes, which is famous for its rich content of organic acids, minerals, tannins and aromatic substances. Drinking red wine regularly (in small amounts) has been shown to reduce the risk of heart disease.

Georgian cuisine

Georgian cuisine is considered to be very spicy. The first thing is hot pepper.

It is no coincidence that Georgians really love to grow and add different types of hot peppers to their food. But not all of them like very spicy dishes. After all, Georgian culture and cuisine, as a part of it, consists of regional dishes that are very different from each other.

Those who have visited Georgia at least once know that the west and east of this country are original and different in their customs. For example, in the west they love spicy dishes more than in the east. If the traditional dishes of each region are written out separately, it will not be clear how they can be combined. But this is so, and some dishes have become the property of the whole of Georgia and a part of its intangible culture.

Georgian cuisine, popular dishes, features

Georgian cuisine is primarily not spicy, but spicy. This country is very fond of spices and some dishes are based on them. For example, the famous Adyghe salt, which consists entirely of spices, Kuchmachi is a dish that cannot be imagined without a huge amount of aromatic additives. And in all the others, spices are also welcome, although sometimes you can do without them.

This is what is called a view from the outside. When tourists write reviews, they are not objective. But what unites people who have tried Georgian cuisine is admiration and desire to return to this country again. The dishes are very diverse in their composition and those who did not like kharcho may fall in love with lobio, khachapuri, suluguni.

Georgian dishes are very diverse in their composition. These are meat dishes, the most famous of which will be satsivi and mtsvadi, Georgian shish kebab. Various types of cheeses, where the primacy in popularity belongs to Imeretian cheese and suluguni. Among dairy products, the most popular drink is yogurt, and from baked goods - khachapuri. There are many types of them, depending on the region, they can be round, square or in the form of a month. You can list the dishes for a very long time.

And, of course, what else distinguishes Georgian cuisine from others is a large amount of wine. Quality, local, time-tested and with its own traditions in winemaking, which cannot be found in other countries. Wine, like all dishes, is made with soul. Georgian cuisine tries to preserve its traditions, especially the principle of hospitality.

Lobio

This is one of the most famous Georgian dishes. The basis of the lobio is beans, and it can be made from both grain and green beans. From cereals, preference is given to dark, red and variegated varieties. Light and white are used less. The very name of the dish comes from a variety of legumes called "lobia", from which they used to prefer to cook. She was preferred for taste and yield.

In different regions, this dish is prepared in different ways. A lot of fried onions, herbs, spices, meat, tomato paste, walnuts are added to it. Each housewife has her own recipe, which depends on local and family traditions. The result is a hearty and healthy snack that can be served cold or hot. Below is a classic version of lobio, a very simple and affordable recipe. It nevertheless turns out to be very tasty. The main thing is to choose quality beans for cooking.

Components:

dark red beans - 450 g;
onions - 2-3 pieces (depending on size);
vegetable oil - 50 ml;
lemon juice - 3 tablespoons;
walnuts - 1 cup (peeled);
parsley greens - 1 bunch;
salt

Cooking:

In order for the beans in the lobio to become soft and tender, you must first soak them overnight. And better - for a day or two. A place for this is chosen cool so that the grain does not sour. And the water is constantly being changed for the same reason.

After soaking, the beans increase in volume by 2-3 times. They need to be rinsed and filled with cold water. Put the saucepan on the stove, bring the water to a boil and reduce the gas.

The beans are cooked from 40 minutes to 1.5 hours, depending on the time of soaking and the variety. It is considered cooked if it can be crushed between the fingers.

Lobio tastes better if you add fried onions to it. It is finely chopped and fried in vegetable oil. Onions are spread in a saucepan with beans half an hour before the end of cooking, so that they fully convey the aroma to the dish.

While the beans and onions are being cooked, you need to make a dressing. For this, walnuts are peeled. They need to be chopped in a way convenient for you, it can be a meat grinder or a blender. You can also chop the walnuts with a knife.

Scald the lemon with boiling water and squeeze out the juice, add finely chopped parsley, nuts, vegetable oil and salt. Mix everything thoroughly.

The beans on the lobio are crushed using a conventional crush. It should be patchy and not mash-like.
Add the dressing to the cooled beans and mix everything. It can be served both hot and cold. Garlic and hot peppers are added to the lobio taste.

Ojakhuri

The name of this dish is translated from Georgian as "family". Traditionally, it is served in ketsi, a national dish that looks like a large frying pan with low sides. It is made of red clay, which retains heat for a long time. Sometimes ojakhuri is laid out in small ketsi, similar to a plate. One Georgian legend is associated with Ojakhuri, which is very believable.

One day the head of the family asked his wife to cook meat. She discovered that there was not enough meat for everyone, and added potatoes. At the same time, the hostess tried to make the new dish very tasty and like her husband. She succeeded and the dish was called in a simple way "family". Even his original recipe has been preserved: potatoes and meat are taken in a 1: 1 ratio. Otherwise, it is a simple and quick option for dinner on weekdays.

Components:

potatoes - 1 kg;
pork with a small amount of fat - 1 kg;
onions - 2 pieces;
garlic - 5-6 cloves;
tomato paste - 3 tablespoons;
adjika - 1 tablespoon;
cilantro - 1 bunch;
vegetable oil;
salt

Preparation:

Cut the pork like goulash or thinner, so that the pieces are quickly fried.
Onions and other vegetables for this dish are cut into slices, like an orange. This method is called rustic. In tomatoes, before cutting them, take out the stalk.
Potatoes are taken young or rubbed with a hard sponge on the peel, washed and cut along with the peel. Dry the potatoes on a towel before frying.
Heat the frying pan, pour over non-vegetable oil. Vegetables are laid one after another in the following sequence: potatoes, onions, pork.
Dissolve Adjika in a third of a glass of water, add garlic and spices. Pour into a frying pan, simmer the fried ingredients under the lid, season with salt.
Finely chop the cilantro greens.
When the dish is ready, add the chopped tomatoes and herbs.
Heat, stirring, for 1 minute. Then turn off the gas.
Ojakhuri should be served hot.

Chicken tapaka

This name has stuck even in culinary recipes. The word "tapaka" came from Turkey, it means a dish, and in Georgian it means a frying pan.
During cooking, it is important to flatten the chicken with a weight. Therefore, you need to buy it in a small size. Previously, it was cooked on baking trays over a fire, now in a frying pan. It is taken with a large diameter so that the cut carcass is removed.

Components:

chicken carcass - 1000-1200 g;
tomatoes - 2-3 pieces;
Bulgarian (sweet) pepper - 1 piece;

butter for frying;
vegetable oil for frying;
garlic - 6-7 cloves;
black pepper - 1 teaspoon;
hops-suneli - 1 teaspoon;
some granulated sugar;
salt

Cooking:

Wash the chicken, dry it and cut the keel on the breast, and then open the carcass.

Now you need to fight it off. To do this, the carcass is covered with a film so that splashes do not fly and beat off until it becomes evenly flat. Its thickness in different parts should be approximately the same.

Now the chicken needs to be marinated. To do this, you need to mix tomato puree with spices. The stalks are removed from tomatoes. Now the fruits need to be cut into 2 parts and grated. Sweet peppers are mashed in the same way.

Ground black pepper, hops-suneli, garlic pounded with salt are added to the resulting puree.

The chicken is placed in the sauce. The most convenient way to do this is in a bag that is in the refrigerator for at least 2 hours. You can marinate the carcass overnight.

Dry the chicken a little before frying it.

The same amount of butter and vegetable oil is melted in a frying pan.

Put the carcass in the oil and fry it on one side, then turn it over, reduce the heat and put a press on top.

Cook for at least 20 minutes, then pour the marinade into the pan.

Once it is halved, the tapaka chicken is ready.
It is served with the sauce in which it was stewed.

Khachapuri

Georgia is famous for its khachapuri. These are tortillas stuffed with the famous Georgian cheese. The word "khachapuri" is translated as bread and cheese. The shape of the famous baked goods depends on the region. They are round, square, or half-moon shaped. The dough for tortillas is made on yogurt (fermented milk product) or yeast. Imeretian cheese or suluguni is used as a filling.

The easiest to make are Imeretian khachapuri or in Georgian - imeruli. Previously, they were baked in a special oven, and now - on an ordinary stove, in a frying pan. Cooking is not very difficult, but it requires certain skills from beginners. For cooking, it is not necessary to use Georgian cheese, you can cook it with any hard cheese, such as Russian or Kostroma.

Components for the dough:

flour - 500 g;
warm water - 1 glass;
dry yeast - 1 tablespoon;
vegetable oil - a quarter cup;
granulated sugar - 2 teaspoons;
salt - 1 teaspoon.
Components for the filling:
any cheese - 500-700 g;
egg;

Preparation:

First you need to prepare the yeast dough. For this, granulated sugar must be diluted in water and yeast added there.

Sift flour, but do not use it immediately. Depending on its grade and gluten content, a little more or a little less is required.

Yeast dough can be cooked in a sponge way (when the dough first comes up, then the dough) or unpaired, when all the ingredients are mixed and the dough is sent to a warm place for 40-60 minutes.

In the first case, the dough is more airy. Pour enough flour into the water with yeast and granulated sugar to make a batter.

It needs to be sent to a warm place to be raised.

Then add salt, add the rest of the flour and knead the dough that is not too steep, which sticks a little to your hands.

The dough should be placed in a warm place, covered with cling film or a towel.

When the dough comes up, mix it with half a serving of vegetable oil and put it on the table.

Divide the dough into pieces and cover with a towel to prevent drying out.

For the filling, grate the cheese and mix with the egg.

To prepare khachapuri, roll the dough into a flat cake to the size of the pan. The filling is laid out in the middle (there should be a lot of it).

The dough is pinched on top and the finished cake with cheese inside must be rolled out again to its previous size. This should be done carefully so as not to tear the dough.

The tortilla is fried in a pan on both sides in vegetable or butter.

Gomi

This is how mamalyga is called in Georgia. Earlier, when there was no corn, it was cooked from the grains of a plant called gomi. Now it is made from corn, but the name remains the same. True, unlike other countries, in Georgia this dish is prepared only from white varieties of corn. A special cereal for gomi is called gergili.

Gomi is widespread in the west of the country, where many dishes are prepared from corn. It is brewed for a very long time and has its own cooking secrets. Firstly, such porridge is always prepared without salt. It is fresh and can complement any dish and become a side dish for meat, fish, cheese. If you put a lot of suluguni cheese in gomi, then it will be a new dish, which is also loved in Georgia, elarji.

Components:
gergili - 600 g;

water - how much the cereal will take;
suluguni - 300 g

Cooking:

A special Georgian spoon, which is similar to a spatula, with a long handle, can be useful for cooking gomi.

Rinse gergili, cover with water and put on fire.

Gomi is brewed for a very long time, at least 40 minutes. In this case, the water boils away and must be added over and over again.

During this time, you need to cut the suluguni into slices.
Once the gomi is ready, you need to put it on a plate along with the suluguni.

Chashushuli

The popular Georgian dish Chashushuli means "stew". It is meat (beef, veal, pork, chicken), stewed with a lot of different vegetables. It looks like a very thick soup. Vegetables produce juice, resulting in a delicious sauce. The most commonly used are tomatoes, peppers (sweet and hot), garlic, onions, herbs and spices.

Components:

veal - 800 g;
onions - 3 pieces;
tomatoes - 4 pcs.;
sweet peppers - 2 pieces;
hot pepper - half;
garlic - 3-4 cloves;
black pepper - 1 teaspoon;
cilantro - a bunch;
tarragon;
vegetable oil;
salt

Preparation:

The veal should not be chopped very coarsely so that it cooks quickly.
The meat is spread in a not very hot frying pan so that it does not fry, but lets out the juice.
Then you need to cover the pan with a lid and stew the meat in your own juice.

While the meat is stewing, you need to chop the onion, sweet and hot peppers are not very fine, but not coarse. Onions can be cut into slices in a rustic way.

In the pan where the meat was stewed, pour a little vegetable oil and put the chopped vegetables there. Fry everything with meat until soft.

Season with salt and black pepper.

Cut the tomatoes in half and grate, making mashed potatoes. Mix it with crushed garlic and finely chopped cilantro and tarragon.

Put everything in a frying pan and simmer for 3 minutes in its own juice. If there is little juice, then the addition of tomato juice or diluted tomato paste is allowed.

Chkmeruli

A very tasty Georgian dish. It came from the town of Chkmeri (Shkmeri), which belongs to the Racha region. The recipe appeared relatively recently thanks to one chef. It was originally pre-fried chicken stewed in garlic and milk sauce. It is now allowed to change some of the nuances of the recipe.

For example, you can use cream or sour cream instead of milk. It is not recommended to substitute ghee for ghee as it gives a pleasant creamy aroma to the whole dish. You can stew poultry in a ketsi, a special earthen pan, or in a regular pan or stewpan. You can even bake the dish in the oven.

It is better to take a smaller chicken, the carcass should weigh no more than 1.5 kg. If it is not possible to buy a whole carcass, then you can cook chkmeruli from legs, thighs or fillets. Although the dish turns out to be tastier if it is cooked from a whole bird.

Components:

chicken - 1 carcass (1200 g);
cream 30% - 2 cups;
ghee - 3 tablespoons;
vegetable oil for frying chicken;
garlic - 1 head;
red pepper;
salt

Preparation:

The chicken should be cut into the bone at the front as for the tapac chicken. Rub the carcass with salt and leave for a while.

Heat a frying pan, pour in vegetable oil, add chicken and fry until crisp on both sides.

In a separate bowl (it is better to take a ladle or a small saucepan), melt the ghee and put finely chopped garlic in it. Stir and remove from heat when garlic aroma is felt in the kitchen. No need to fry it until golden brown.

About a minute after laying the garlic, you need to pour milk (cream, sour cream) into this dish. Simmer over very low heat until the sauce thickens.

While the sauce is boiling down, you can cut the chicken. It is cut into 8 pieces.

Now you need to put everything in ketsi and pour the resulting milk sauce.

The chicken is boiled in the sauce for at least half an hour. You can use another option: send it to bake in the oven at 180-190 degrees for 20 minutes. If you turn on the grill function, a beautiful crust will form on top.

Chanakhi

The word “chanakhi” is translated from Georgian as “roast”, which is cooked in a pot. Lamb pieces are stewed with vegetables. By weight, they should be the same as meat. The most commonly used vegetables are eggplants, tomatoes, potatoes, onions. All ingredients are placed in layers, sometimes beans and cereals are added to the dish to give it thickness and satiety. In modern cuisine, lamb is often replaced by beef, pork, or poultry.

Components:

fatty pork - 500 g;
potatoes - 2 medium;
eggplant - 1 piece;
tomatoes - 2 pcs.;
onions - 1-2 pieces;
walnuts - 0.5 cups;
garlic - 2 cloves;
hot pepper - half;
greens - a bunch;
salt

Preparation:

Cut the onion into half rings, finely garlic, and hot pepper into small pieces.

Pork should be taken with a layer of lard so that the ingredients can be fried on this fat. Chop the meat into portions and fry a lot to obtain a beautiful crust.

Add onion, garlic and pepper to the pork, fry everything.

Once golden brown, add water and cover.
While everything is stewing, you need to prepare other foods.
Preheat the oven to 180 degrees.

Chop the walnuts.

Potatoes, eggplant, tomatoes are cut into cubes. Sprinkle the eggplants with salt to release the bitterness. After 10-15 minutes, they are washed with water.
Finely chop the greens.

All the products are stacked in a pot in layers: pork with onions and garlic below, eggplant, potatoes, tomato, herbs. Top with broth, formed after stewing meat.

Place in the oven for 40 minutes. Serve in a pot.

Georgian Khinkali

According to one of the beautiful legends, Georgian khinkali was invented by a loving mountain woman. In order to stay longer with her beloved, she came up with a dish where you have to chop meat with a knife for a long time, then wrap it in dough, carefully forming an endless number of identical folds.

The young man chopped fresh mutton himself, with the help of a dagger. Then he sat and waited for the beauty to prepare food ... But the wait was worth it. Beautiful "bags" with juicy meat inside, mixed with aromatic mountain herbs, served from the hands of a beautiful girl, soon became a national dish of Georgian cuisine. There is another version of the origin of khinkali. But more about her later.

Features of khinkali

If someone thinks that khinkali are the same dumplings, only larger and look different, then he is deeply mistaken. The difference is huge.

It's not about the filling, where a special set of spices is added, and not about the dough, which needs to be kneaded for a particularly long time and thoroughly. And not that meat for khinkali is chopped, and not twisted in a meat grinder. There is a third component in it, the most important, for the sake of which this whole venture is: meat broth. It is formed during cooking, inside the bag, where juice flows from the juicy meat. The more juice, the more joy the hostess has: it means that the dish has turned out!

Khinkali is boiled in a large amount of water. They must not be allowed to stick together, stick to the bottom, or be digested. The broth will run out, the idea of the dish will disappear.

Filling for khinkali

Today it is permissible to make khinkali not only from mutton, but also from beef and pork. An excellent filling is obtained if you mix lamb and beef, the second option is beef plus pork.

Another indispensable filling product is onions. If you want to find out how many onions should be put into khinkali according to the rules, the answer will be: the more, the better. Garlic should be added in moderation.

What spices give khinkali a peculiar aroma? First of all, it is ground black pepper. There is one clarification here. This is not the kind of pepper that is sold in "powder". Keep it fresh and of good quality; khinkali requires coarsely ground black pepper. The peas can simply be crushed in a mortar without passing them through the mill.

Popular spices include suneli hops, coriander, and red ground pepper. In any proportion, they are compatible with each other.

There is no filling for khinkali without finely chopped greens. Today housewives add dill. Indeed, it gives a good taste to the dish. But you can do without dill. But without twigs of cilantro and basil, khinkali will not have a "signature" aroma. Parsley and green onion feathers will not spoil the taste of the dish.

On a note:

There is another interesting herb that is actively used in Georgian cuisine: kondari (another name for savory). It is added to many Caucasian meat and fish dishes, including khinkali. The herb is fragrant and requires a small amount. Savory, like all other spices and herbs, has a special taste and beneficial effect on the human body.

The secret of delicious dough

The subject of the eternal debate of housewives: is it necessary to add an egg to the dough? We will not offend the ryaba chicken, but the egg is an absolutely unnecessary product in the khinkali dough. Despite the well-established opinion that the dough will break without an egg, in this case it is not necessary! Miraculously, the "bags" with broth and minced meat will not creep and break during cooking. The egg will add the taste of "egg noodles" to the dish. During cooking, the dough will not be able to absorb the required portion of meat broth; at the exit, the product will be tough.

The secret lies in good wheat flour of the highest or first grade and long kneading of the dough to a soft, fluffy, but at the same time elastic state. The young man, who was waiting for the mountain woman to knead the dough, had tremendous patience.

So, the dough for khinkali is prepared from three products: flour, water and salt.

On a note:

If you want to get a high-quality product at the end, everything must be of high quality at all stages. This also applies to water. In the city it will not be possible to scoop up from a mountain spring, so it is better to take boiled, soft water. The dough will turn out to be elastic, it will stretch well without tearing.

Cooking technology in stages

Today there are many recipes for cooking this dish. There is no doubt that only in Georgia you can taste real khinkali made from mountain lamb meat with the addition of original spices. The main task is to find tasty, high-quality meat and not spare spices and herbs. You should maintain the proportions of products and take your time during the cooking process.

The composition and quantity of products :

lamb and beef meat in equal proportions - 1000 grams;
onion - 2 large or 4 medium size;
wheat flour - 1000 grams;
salt - a teaspoon for the dough, in the filling - to taste;
greens - 3-4 bunches (cilantro, parsley, dill, basil, savory - at choice or all together)
spices (black coarsely ground pepper - required, hops-suneli, red hot ground pepper, coriander - optional);
garlic is a big head
drinking water - 500 grams for kneading dough and 3 liters for cooking khinkali;
This amount of products is enough to eat by yourself and put the dish on the table for guests.

How to make the filling

chop the meat thoroughly;
finely chop the onion;
peel and crush garlic;
chop greens;
mix all the ingredients, adding salt to taste and a tablespoon of ground black pepper;
beat off the mixture so that the khinkali subsequently “melt” in the mouth (lift the mass up and forcefully throw it back into the bowl);
pour a glass of warm boiled water into the resulting filling (do not interfere, let it absorb).
After that, give the filling "rest" for half an hour, at this time do the dough.

How to make dough

In khinkali, dough is not just a "wrapper" for meat, it is tasty in itself and great importance is attached to the quality of the dough.

Cooking:

pour a pile of flour on the table, make a depression in the middle;
mix warm water with salt;
pour the saline solution into the center of the slide in a thin stream, stir with a fork, grabbing the flour from the sides of the groove for as long as possible;
switch to manual kneading;
knead the dough in 3-4 stages, adding flour and letting it "breathe" for about 10 minutes.
The result should be a soft, "springy" ball.

On a note:

You may need more or less a kilogram of flour. It depends on its quality characteristics.

How to sculpt and cookheated

A large pot of salted water can already be on the stove. Throw in a couple of bay leaves and start sculpting.

The most convenient way:

divide the dough into several 4-5 parts in order to gradually cook khinkali in small portions;
roll out thinly one layer of dough on the table; squeeze out circles with a bowl or mug with a diameter of 10-12 cm;
lay out the filling in a circle and immediately carefully collect the "sides" in a heap, while making the most even folds;
immerse khinkali in water in small portions;
after 2-3 minutes, carefully lift the "bags" from the bottom so that they do not stick (no need to interfere);
After surfacing, cook for no more than 5-6 minutes over low heat.
Remove with a slotted spoon, put on a dish, sprinkle immediately with ground hot pepper.
Different sauces are served on request.

Khinkali is cooked in parts. When the water in the pan is noticeably reduced (the dough absorbs), you should add more. Salt, wait until it boils again, and only then add a new portion.

On a note:

Sculpting beautiful khinkali is an art that needs to be learned. If you manage to make more than 15 even folds - this is a great success, and you can stop there.

They eat khinkali with their hands. Take by the "tail" and carefully bite the dough in such a way as to drink the broth. 5-6 pieces are enough to feel full and energized. Mountain peoples used this property in ancient times to replenish the strength of wounded soldiers. They say that is why the khinkali has such a shape - in the form of a traveling knapsack.

"Pouches" were baked over a fire, under a crispy crust there was a delicious healing mutton broth and meat.

Satsebeli

It is impossible to imagine Georgian cuisine without satsebeli (or satsibeli) sauce. It is believed to be a classic barbecue seasoning. With a hot, spicy sauce, heavy foods are better absorbed by the body. In addition to the benefits, the bright taste of satsebel is of great importance. It is spicy, fragrant and goes very well with meat.

The classic Georgian satsebeli is very spicy. Therefore, if you are not used to such food, you need to reduce the amount of garlic and hot peppers. The sauce contains enough acid and various natural preservatives such as hot peppers, salt, and garlic. Therefore, it can be prepared for future use in the fall, when there are a lot of vegetables: tomatoes, peppers, garlic.

Real satsebeli is made from sweet varieties of tomatoes. They should not be light and unripe. It is better if the vegetables are already soft and overripe.

For the dish you need:

2 kg of ripe tomatoes;
1 kg of sweet bell pepper;
red hot peppers to taste;
1 tablespoon (with a slide) utskho-suneli;
1 heaping teaspoon of ground coriander seeds
salt to taste.

Preparation:

The sauce is prepared in a special dish. It is better for this purpose to take a cauldron, a stewpan, a saucepan or a deep frying pan with a thick bottom so that the satsebeli does not burn.

Washed vegetables: tomatoes and 2 types of peppers are cut into large pieces, cutting out the green stalks.

Everything is laid out in a saucepan, at the bottom of which a little water is poured so that the vegetables do not burn. In the future, the tomatoes will release their juice and will be stewed in it.

The container is placed on the stove, first on a strong fire. Then, after boiling, it decreases.

Vegetables are simmered over low heat for at least half an hour, until they become very soft and turn into gruel.
The whole mass is wiped through a sieve and put on fire again so that the liquid evaporates a little.

Now you can add salt to taste, utskho-suneli and freshly ground coriander.
It remains to bring the satsebeli to the desired consistency by boiling it for 5 minutes.

Satsebeli from tomato paste to kebabs

Satsebeli (or satsibeli) has many recipes that everyone adapts for himself and his family. One of them, from tomato paste, is prepared in winter or spring. When you want to try real Georgian satsebeli, tomatoes are too expensive. For this sauce, you need to choose a good quality pasta, which is made from tomatoes without adding dyes and flavors.

For the dish you need:

400 g of tomato paste;
Satsebeli is a classic Georgian recipe for
2-3 teaspoons of adjika (paste);
350-400 ml of water;
a lot, 2-3 bunches, cilantro;
1-2 heads of garlic (focus on your taste);
half a teaspoon of black ground pepper;
2 tablespoons (with a slide) hops-suneli;
1 tablespoon vinegar
salt to taste

Preparation:

Tomato paste must be mixed with adjika, black pepper, hop-suneli seasoning, vinegar.

We do not need cilantro stalks, and the leaves must be finely chopped. You can use the help of a blender, but this is not at all necessary.

Chop the garlic in any convenient way: grind with salt, grate on a fine grater, squeeze through a press.

Now the herbs and garlic must be mixed with tomato paste.

Now is the time to dilute the mixture with water and bring it to the consistency of a regular sauce. You do not need to immediately pour out the entire amount of water indicated in the recipe.
Tomato paste can have different densities and thicknesses.

Salt also needs to be done carefully, because the purchased adjika can contain a large amount of salt. After salt, you need to wait until the salt dissolves, and only then add salt.

The sauce is ready. But not really: to make it tastier, it must be placed in the refrigerator for at least an hour. And it is better if it stands in a cool place under a lid for 8-12 hours.

This sauce can be used with dumplings, fried meat, fish, cabbage rolls, or as a spicy addition to soups and hot dishes.

Satsebeli: the easiest option

This satsebeli option is not the fastest. To prepare it, you need to peel and boil the tomatoes. And it takes a long time. But in terms of the quantity and availability of the main ingredients, it is the easiest. Maybe this is exactly what you like. And by the way, it's not too sharp.

For the dish you need:

1 kg of ripe tomatoes;
red pepper (sweet paprika);
1 teaspoon of hops-suneli;
1 teaspoon ground black pepper
3 cloves of garlic;
salt to taste

Preparation:

Cut the tomatoes crosswise near the stalk and place for a few seconds in boiling water. Remove the skin, cut out the green stalk and place in a container with a thick bottom.

Pour in a little (no more than a glass) water and put on fire. Before boiling, sometimes you need to stir the tomatoes, and then close the lid and put on the slowest heat for 40 minutes.

If the mass is not homogeneous enough, then you can connect the help of a blender and puree the mixture.
Without turning off the gas, add salt, pepper, sweet paprika and suneli hops to the paste.

The mixture must be brought to the desired density by evaporating the liquid. Do not forget that when cooled down, the sauce will be thicker.

Squeeze the garlic through a press and dip in the hot sauce just before turning off.

This sauce is also best kept in the refrigerator for a couple of hours. It turns out to be spicy, with a slight edge. It can be eaten simply by spreading it on bread, dipping a cake or pita bread into it.

Satsebeli: the fastest version

This sauce is very fast. It is suitable for those who want an authentic version in a short time!

For the dish you need:

300-400 g of tomato paste;
a large bunch of cilantro;
1-2 tablespoons of adjika;
salt to taste;
water
satsebeli classic Georgian recipe

Preparation:

Finely chop the cilantro, mix it with tomato paste.
Add water to create the consistency of the sauce.
Add Adjika to taste.
At the very end, add salt to the sauce.
This sauce takes 5-10 minutes to cook. If you have chosen high-quality pasta and good adjika, then the result will be excellent!

Armenian Cuisine

Armenian culinary traditions are very ancient, and many customs have remained unchanged for several thousand years. The dishes are spicy and spicy, very aromatic and with a lot of vegetables. They are usually served with pita bread baked in a clay oven tonir.

Armenian culinary traditions date back to ancient times. It is known that the Armenians had an idea of the processes of fermentation and baking 2500 years ago. The traditions of cooking many Armenian dishes remain unchanged.

The tradition and continuity of Armenian cuisine is manifested in different ways - for example, in the use of ancient kitchen utensils and in the technology of cooking.

The names of many dishes of Armenian cuisine are associated with the name of the dishes in which they are prepared, for example: putuk, kchuch, tapak.

Kyufta

Balls of chopped and boiled meat with spices.

Ingredients:

- 700 g of beef,
- 1 onion,
- spices,
- 50 ml of milk,
- 50 ml of brandy,
- 100 ml of red wine,
- 50 g of butter,
- herbs

Preparation:

Pass the meat through a meat grinder several times, add spices, brandy, milk and chopped onion. Mix everything well and form large balls. Add wine to boiling water, boil balls in it, cut and serve with herbs and butter.

Amich

Poultry stuffed with rice and dried fruits.

Ingredients:

- 1 chicken,
- 0.5 cups of almonds,
- 5 dates,
- 75 g butter,
- 1/4 cup each dried apricots and raisins,
- 1 tsp each. cinnamon and ground cloves,
- 0.5 cups of rice,
- salt,
- herbs

Preparation:

Boil rice until half cooked and fry in a spoonful of butter. Soak dried fruits for 10 minutes and chop together with nuts. Fry them separately in 2 tbsp. oils. Combine rice, herbs, dried fruits and spices and stuff the washed chicken. Lightly fry it on each side, put it in a mold, brush with oil, pour in 0.5 cups of water and put in the oven for 45 minutes at 180 degrees.

Vegetable khorovats

Salad made from baked vegetables.

Ingredients:

4 eggplants,
5 tomatoes,
5 peppers,
1 onion,
3 tbsp. vegetable oil,
spices

Preparation:

Rinse all vegetables except onions and bake them whole in the oven until tender. Chop everything into small cubes and add chopped onions, herbs, spices and oil to taste.

Kololak

Round meatballs are boiled in tomato broth.

Ingredients:

- 300 g of beef on the bone,
- 3 potatoes,
- 1 tbsp. tomato paste,
- 0.5 cups of rice,
- herbs,
- spices,
- 300 g minced meat,
- 3 tbsp. millet,
- 2 onions.

Preparation:

Boil the broth and the meat and add the potato sticks to it. Add onion, spices and boiled millet to the minced meat. Mix the cooked rice with herbs and spices separately. Shape meatballs with rice filling and place in hot soup. Add tomato paste there and boil for another 7 minutes.

Tzhvzhik

Armenian roast from offal with spices, herbs and vegetables.

Ingredients:

- 800 g of liver, stomachs and other offal,
- 200 g of onions,
- 30 ml of red wine,
- herbs,
- butter

Preparation:

Cut the offal into strips and fry in melted butter for about 7 minutes. Add spices and wine and continue to simmer until tender. Sprinkle with herbs before serving.

Dolma Cabbage

Lamb or beef rolls in grape leaves.

Ingredients:

- 1.3 kg beef,
- 150 g tomatoes,
- half sweet pepper,
- 650 g grape leaves,
- 9 tbsp. butter,
- spices,
- basil,
- cilantro,

- hot pepper,
- paprika,
- 8 tbsp. basmati rice,

Preparation:

Pour boiling water over the grape leaves for 10 minutes. Pass the meat with vegetables and butter through a meat grinder. Add raw rice, herbs, spices to the minced meat and mix well. Wrap the filling in leaves, but not too tightly, place in dense rows in a saucepan, cover with water and cook under the lid for about 40 minutes after simmering over low heat.

Arisa

Wheat porridge with chicken and butter.

Ingredients:

500 g millet,
600 g chicken,
75 g butter,
2 liters of water,
salt

Preparation:

Boil the chicken, remove from the broth and chop the meat. During this time, put the washed millet in the broth. Return the chicken back and simmer for 3-4 hours over low heat, stirring occasionally. At the end, salt and add butter.

Zhengyalov Haz

Bread flatbread stuffed with greens.

Ingredients:

- 450 g flour,
- 270 ml water,
- vegetable oil,
- salt,
- 60-90 g each green onion,
- lettuce,
- spinach,
- sorrel,

- beet leaves,
- cilantro,
- parsley,
- dill and nettle

Preparation:

Knead the dough with flour, salt, water and 2 tbsp. vegetable oil. Leave it on for half an hour, but for now grind all the greens. Divide the dough into pieces, roll into thin cakes, lay out the filling and pinch the edges. Fry the cakes in a dry frying pan on both sides.

Tsitsak

Great Armenian hot pepper for the winter.

Ingredients:

- 500 g of hot peppers,
- 20 g of dill,
- 3 cloves of garlic,
- 20 g of salt,
- 1 liter of water

Preparation:

Put a layer of chopped dill and garlic in a container, put pepper, and alternate layers. Fill everything with water and salt and leave it under a press in a cool place for 1.5-2 weeks. When the pepper turns yellow, the tsitsi can be put in jars.

Mshosh

Lentils with dried fruits and nuts.

Ingredients:

- 0.5 cups lentils,
- 1 tbsp. vegetable oil,
- half an onion,
- dried apricots, prunes,
- crushed walnuts,
- herbs and spices to taste

Preparation:

Boil the lentils until almost cooked and add the fried onions to it. Add nuts, dried fruits and spices there, boil for another 15 minutes, and sprinkle with herbs.

Hapama

Pumpkin is one of the main and most versatile vegetables in Armenian cuisine.

Ingredients:

- 1 pumpkin (2 kg),
- 1 onion,
- 100 g raisins,
- 50 g rice,
- 50 g walnuts,
- 100 g butter,

- 1 tsp. cinnamon

Preparation:

Cut off the top of the pumpkin and remove the pulp.

Fry chopped onions in a little butter, add rice and fry until golden brown.

Soak raisins in boiling water, chop nuts and pumpkin pulp, and add everything with spices to onions and rice.

Fill the pumpkin with 150 ml of water, cover with the top and cook for 2 hours in the oven at 170 degrees.

Bozbash

Armenian hearty meat soup with vegetables and tomato dressing.

Ingredients:

- 300 g lamb,
- 0.5 cups chickpeas,
- 2 onions,
- 1 tbsp. butter and tomato paste,
- 2 potatoes,

- 1 apple,
- 0.5 cups of prunes,
- 1 tbsp. lemon juice,
- Spices

Preparation:

Soak the chickpeas in advance overnight.

Coarsely chop the lamb, boil for an hour after boiling, remove from the pan and put the chickpeas in the broth.

After 20 minutes, add the fried onion with tomato paste in butter and the rest of the ingredients.

Boil everything together for another 10 minutes, season with lemon juice and spices, and let it brew for 20 minutes.

Spas

Original soup without meat based on yogurt and millet. Can be served hot or cold.

Ingredients:

- 800 g yogurt,
- 1 liter of water,
- 1 can of sour cream,
- 2 tbsp. flour,
- 1 egg,
- 1.5 cups of millet,
- 1 onion, spices

Preparation:

Mix flour, salt, egg and millet, and separately mix yogurt, sour cream and water. Combine both masses, stir so that there are no lumps, and put on a small fire. Cook, stirring occasionally, until desired consistency and season.

Khash

The most popular Armenian soup is traditionally eaten for breakfast.

Ingredients:

- 1.5 kg of beef leg,
- 500 g of beef tripe,
- 3 heads of garlic,
- 1 radish

Preparation:

Pour the washed and chopped leg with water so that it covers it by 20 cm, and cook. Separately boil the scars until the odor disappears, rinse, chop and add to the legs. Continue cooking until the meat is completely tender. Add chopped garlic at the end. Serve with grated radish.

Imam Bayildi

Spicy and aromatic eggplant appetizer.

Ingredients:

- 3 eggplants,
- 1 onion,
- 2 tomatoes,
- half a pepper,
- 2 cloves of garlic,
- herbs,
- 5 tbsp. olive oil,
- spices.

Preparation:

Cut the eggplants into thin layers and cover with water and salt for 40 minutes.
Chop onions with garlic, herbs, peppers and peeled tomatoes.
Fry the eggplants until golden, and fry the onions separately with the rest of the ingredients.
Put everything in layers in sterilized jars.

Barurik

A crumbly roll that slightly resembles baklava in taste and texture.

Ingredients:

- 1 cup flour,
- 0.5 cups walnuts,
- 120 g butter,
- 0.5 cups sugar,
- 1 egg,
- cinnamon

Preparation:

Knead half of the softened butter, flour and egg into a dough and leave to rest for 20 minutes.
Mix chopped nuts with sugar and cinnamon.
Roll out the dough in a layer, lay out the filling, roll the roll, brush it with butter and bake for 15-20 minutes at 220 degrees.

Gata

Lush Armenian flatbread with butter and flour filling.

Ingredients:

- 100 g butter,
- 500 g flour, 100 ml milk,
- 1 tsp. dry yeast,
- 2 eggs,
- 1 tsp. vanilla sugar,
- 4 tablespoons sugar, a
- pinch of salt,

- 200 g of butter in the filling,
- 1 glass of powdered sugar

Preparation:

Add yeast to warm milk, mix with flour and leave warm for half an hour.

Beat eggs with sugar and butter, and add to the dough with salt. Leave it on for another 40 minutes.

Mix the remaining flour with powdered sugar and vanilla sugar, and gradually add ghee for the filling.

Divide the dough into three parts, roll out, spread out the filling and tighten the edges. Shape and roll the gata again, brush with butter and yolks, and bake at 180 degrees for half an hour.

Alani

Sun-dried peaches with sweet and spicy nut filling.

Ingredients:

10 dried peaches,
nuts, dried fruits,

powdered sugar and honey.

Preparation:

Chop nuts and dried fruits and stir with honey and powdered sugar to taste. Fill the dried peaches with a mass and leave for half an hour.

Matnakash

A classic recipe for Armenian bread in the oven.

Ingredients:

- 2 tbsp. sour cream,
- 400 ml of water,
- 7 g of dry yeast,
- 550 g of flour,
- salt,
- 20 g of sugar,
- 60 ml of vegetable oil

Preparation:

Heat 100 ml of water, add sour cream, sugar and yeast to it, and leave for 15 minutes.

Pour the yeast and the remaining water into the flour and salt, knead the dough and add the butter at the end.

The dough needs to be kneaded for about 20 minutes, and then left until it triples in volume.

Divide the dough into two flat cakes, roll out, make grooves-holes, brush with water and butter and bake for 10-15 minutes in the oven at maximum temperature.

Azerbaijani cuisine

Azerbaijani national food is distinguished by a great variety, numbering dozens of different types of dishes: dairy, meat, flour, vegetable, etc. The methods of cooking and consumption of food themselves are different and varied. In the past, food also differed depending on the geographical conditions and social status of people.

Shish kebabs and dishes in tandoor were widely used in Azerbaijani cuisine. There are various drinks, sweets. A distinctive feature of Azerbaijani cuisine is the use of lamb for cooking various dishes. To a much lesser extent, Azerbaijanis consume beef, poultry, and fish. The formation of Azerbaijani cuisine was influenced by the requirements of Islam - as a result, pork dishes and dishes containing alcohol are traditionally not presented in it. Another feature of Azerbaijani cuisine is a pungent taste and unique aroma, which give the dishes all kinds of spices and herbs: bitter and allspice, basil, cinnamon, cloves, dill, parsley, cilantro, mint, cumin and many others. It is especially worth dwelling on saffron and sumac.

The first of them is an indispensable component for the preparation of numerous pilafs. Sumakh is usually served with various meat dishes. Azerbaijani cuisine widely uses vegetables (tomatoes, cucumbers, eggplants and others), fruits (apples, pears, quince, oranges, lemons), stone fruits (plums, cherry plums, apricots, peaches). There are also various types of dolma made from eggplant, tomato and pepper.

Kutabs with potatoes and cheese

Dough:

- Water - 250 ml
- Flour - 600-650 g
- Salt - 1 tsp
- Vegetable oil - 1 tbsp

Filling:

- Pickled cheese (any) - 200 g
- Potatoes - 4 pcs.

- Green onion - 50 g
- Dill - 30 g
- Butter - 30 g
- Butter - for lubrication

To prepare the dough for kutabs, we will take all the products stated in the list.

Knead a dense dough from water, salt, butter and flour.

Combine water, butter and flour.

Cover the dough with a towel and leave to ripen while the filling is cooking.

Knead the dough.

To prepare the filling, take the following ingredients:

The proportions are arbitrary, what you want more, then put it.

Boil potatoes in salted water.

Put potatoes in water.

Crumble or finely chop the cheese.

Chop the cheese.

Drain the water from the boiled potatoes and mash them in mashed potatoes, adding butter.

Grind the potatoes.

Then add the chopped herbs and cheese. Season with salt and pepper, stir well.

Add herbs and cheese.

Take a portion of the dough, roll it into a rope and cut into equal pieces.
Divide the dough into pieces.

Flatten each piece into a flat cake and roll thinly so that the dough shines through. Put the filling in a thin layer on one side.

Place the filling on the dough.

Cover with the other side of the tortillas and press firmly, expelling the air. Trim the edges of the dough with a wheel. When frying, the cheese will melt and the filling will become smooth.

Cut off excess dough.

Put the finished kutabs on a tray sprinkled with flour. They can also be frozen for future use and stored in the freezer until needed, wrapped in a plastic bag or folded into a container.

Blind the kutabs.

Fry the kutabs on both sides in a dry frying pan and stack them on top of each other.

Fry kutabs.

Be sure to grease the surface with butter.

Kutabs with potatoes and cheese are ready.

Serve with mint tea or fermented milk sauces.

Chikhirtma

Chikhirtma from chicken is a very tasty, tender and satisfying dish of Azerbaijani cuisine. Chykhyrtma is served as a side dish for folding pilaf, but it is also very tasty as an independent dish. The chicken turns out to be very tender and fragrant, the onion-tomato sauce is very harmonious, and the addition of eggs makes chikhirtma a delicious dish!

Ingredients:

- Chicken - 600 g
- Onions - 400 g
- Chicken eggs - 3 pcs.
- Butter - 70 g
- Vegetable oil - 2 tbsp.
- Tomato (large) - 1 pc.
- Lemon juice - 2 tablespoons

- Turmeric - 1 tsp
- Chicken broth (water) - 1 tbsp.
- Salt, pepper - to taste
- Greens - to taste

Preparation:

First, put the chicken to boil, because we also need chicken broth.

Meanwhile, peel and finely chop the onion.

Do not worry that there are too many onions - onions simmered in oil will become the basis of a wonderful sauce.

onion

Chop theMelt the butter in a deep frying pan or in a saucepan, put the onion. 5-7 minutes, stirring occasionally, we will simmer the onion in oil,
not letting it fry. Salt a little.

Fry the onion.

Meanwhile, remove the skin from the tomato, making an incision and holding it in boiling water for a minute, and chop finely.

Chop the tomatoes.

Add the chopped tomato to the onion, mix and simmer together for 2-3 minutes.

Put tomatoes on the onion.

Our chicken has been cooked, take out the pieces from the broth and, if desired, fry a little.

Boil the chicken.

In the onion-tomato mixture, add the juice of half a lemon and pour in 1/3 cup of broth.

Pour in water.

Now put the chicken in the pan.

Put chicken in the pan.
Add a little salt and add 1 tsp. turmeric for color and flavor.

Pour in salt and turmeric.

Pour the remaining broth, close the lid and simmer the chicken with vegetables for 20-25 minutes over medium heat. If necessary, top up with a little broth,so that the onions don't cook. Finely chop the greens.

Chop the onion.

Beat the eggs with a fork, add a little salt and pepper. Remember that we have already salted the onions and chicken.

Beat eggs with salt and pepper.

Pour the eggs into the pan, trying to spread the mixture over the entire surface, between the chicken pieces.

Cover with a lid and cook for 2-3 minutes so that the eggs "grab".

You cannot stir, you can only pierce the omelet so that it cooks evenly.

Pour eggs into the chicken.

That's all, chicken chyhyryn is ready! You can serve it with a side dish of rice, for example, butas an independent
it is also a very tasty dish! Sprinkle with herbs and serve immediately.

Deliciously tender chicken in onion sauce and tomato, with tender omelet and herbs -

that's what chyhyryn is.

Kufta-bozbash

Kufta-bozbash is an unusually tasty thick soup with large stuffed meatballs from lamb or beef meat. The recipe for this soup came from the era of the rule of the Ottoman Empire, I liked it and is popular to the present.

There are many recipes for making this soup. In each region, when preparing kufta-bozbash, there may be slight deviations from the main recipe and additions from your favorite spices. Even the family in the neighborhood can cook this soup in their own way. But always and everywhere the basis will be minced lamb or beef minced through a meat grinder, chickpeas and herbs.

If you are going to cook kufta-bozbash in Azerbaijani, then soak chickpeas in water for at least 3 hours.

Ingredients:

Minced lamb - 500 g
Salt - to taste
Basil (dried) - 2 tbsp.
Cherry plum (dried apricots, prunes) - 4 pcs.
Turmeric - 1 tsp
Potatoes - 2 pcs.
Chickpeas - 0.5 cups
Onions for minced meat - 1 pc.
Onions for frying - 1 pc.
Rice - 50 g
Dried dill, dried mint - to taste
Ground chili pepper - 1/4 tsp.

Preparation:

Put the chickpeas in a saucepan, pour in water, salt to taste and cook for about 30 minutes.

Boil the chickpeas.

While the chickpeas are boiling, prepare the minced meat for the "kyufta" (large meatballs).

Place the minced meat in a bowl. I have a mixture of beef and lamb fat.

Make the minced meat.

Add finely chopped onions, hot chili peppers, dried basil, salt and rice to the minced meat. In some families, rice is not put, but instead boiled and chopped chickpeas are added.

Add spices and rice.

Form large meatballs from the minced meat. Moreover, in size they should be like a fist.

In the middle of each meatball, put the dried fruits you have: cherry plum (ideally), prunes, dried apricots.

Form meatballs with prunes.

In the finished chickpea broth, add potatoes cut into large quarters.

Add potatoes to the chickpeas.

And immediately add the cufta balls.

Put the meatballs.

It remains to make the frying. Simply sauté the finely chopped onion in vegetable oil and add the turmeric to it.

Ideally, if you have saffron, then this is exactly the dish where it would go perfectly.

Fry the onion with spices.

Pour the frying into the soup and without stirring, so as not to violate the integrity of the kyufta, cook the soup over very low heat until the potatoes are ready. This is about 15-20 minutes.

Put the frying in the soupstyle.

When the Azerbaijani-kyufta-bozbash is ready, add dried herbs: mint, basil and dill.

Add spices to the soup The soup is ready! Enjoy your meal!

Shah-pilaf

Shah-pilaf is a dish of Azerbaijani cuisine, it is cooked in the oven in the form of a pilaf pie wrapped in lavash. It turns out to be a very interesting and tasty dish, a real work of culinary creativity. Usually shah-pilaf in Azerbaijani style (in lavash) is made from chicken.

Ingredients:

- Chicken drumsticks - 300 g
- Round grain rice for pilaf - 150 glavash

- Thin- 1 pc.
- Onions - 0.5 pcs.
- Carrots - 0.5 pcs.
- Dried apricots - 50 g
- Raisins - 50 g
- Garlic - 3 cloves
- Turmeric - 1 pinch
- Saffron - on the tip of a knife
- Spices for pilaf - 1 pinch
- Butter - 50 g
- Salt - 1 tsp.

Preparation:

To prepare the royal Azerbaijani Shah-pilaf in lavash in a cauldron, take chicken drumsticks, round-grain rice for pilaf, onions, carrots, dried apricots, raisins, garlic, turmeric, saffron, spices for pilaf, butter, salt.

Cook rice in the microwave, add oil, pour raisins and dried apricots with boiling water.

Pour rice and dried fruits with water.

Cut meat, carrots, onions.

Chop onions, carrots and meat.

Fry everything in hot oil in a cauldron.

Fry onions and carrots with meat.

Chop dried apricots, rinse the raisins well, remove the seeds.

Cut dried fruits.

Add fruits and spices to the cauldron.

Add dried fruits and spices.

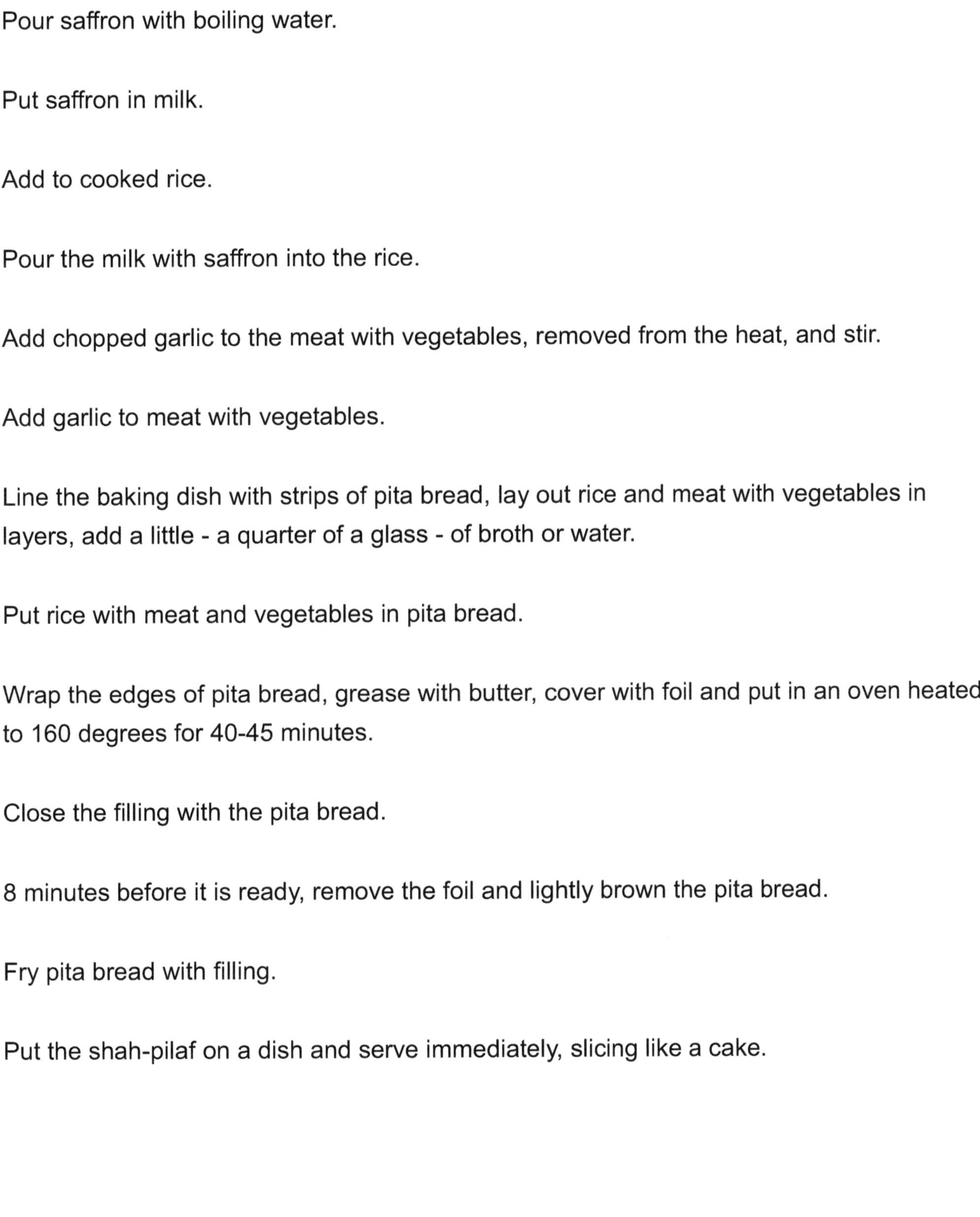

Pour saffron with boiling water.

Put saffron in milk.

Add to cooked rice.

Pour the milk with saffron into the rice.

Add chopped garlic to the meat with vegetables, removed from the heat, and stir.

Add garlic to meat with vegetables.

Line the baking dish with strips of pita bread, lay out rice and meat with vegetables in layers, add a little - a quarter of a glass - of broth or water.

Put rice with meat and vegetables in pita bread.

Wrap the edges of pita bread, grease with butter, cover with foil and put in an oven heated to 160 degrees for 40-45 minutes.

Close the filling with the pita bread.

8 minutes before it is ready, remove the foil and lightly brown the pita bread.

Fry pita bread with filling.

Put the shah-pilaf on a dish and serve immediately, slicing like a cake.

Chicken Buglama

The national dish of Azerbaijan is the first and second in one plate at once.
Buglama is a well-known and popular dish in Azerbaijan, it is the first and second at once, so it is very profitable to cook it for holidays and family dinners.

"Buglama" in translation means "cooked in its own juice", something like this, I could be wrong.

Usually in Azerbaijan they prepare buglama from fish or lamb, but it is not very popular with chicken. Yes, this, in fact, is not a dish, but a method of preparation, so nothing prevents us from making it our own way and preparing it from chicken.

Mandatory and essential products for making buglama are meat or fish, bell peppers, tomatoes, onions and herbs.

Ingredients:

Chicken thighs without bone - 1 kg
Bulgarian pepper - 600 g
Onions - 500 g
Tomatoes - 500 g
Ghee butter - 1 tbsp.
Parsley - 30 g
Basil - 10 g
Salt - to taste
Pepper h.m. - to taste
Hot pepper - to taste

Preparation:

So, prepare the necessary ingredients for making chicken buglama in Azerbaijani style.

Take a thick-walled cauldron or duck. Since chicken thighs in this case do not have their own fat, add butter to the bottom of the cauldron. Put all products in a cold cauldron.

The first layer is onion half rings. Put not the whole onion, but the third part.

Next, lay half the chicken meat in an even layer on top of the onion, and then again half the onion rings. Salt, pepper, add hot pepper, if you like hot. I also always add my favorite seasoning to all dishes - a mixture of spices khmeli-suneli, I do not indicate it in the ingredients, since it is usually not used in Azerbaijan. But turmeric is often sprinkled on meat, and we are not lovers of it.

Spread the pieces of bell pepper further. Sprinkle a little salt and pepper on each layer.

Then - again a layer of chicken meat. Let's not forget about salt and pepper.

Alternate layers. After the chicken - again onions and bell peppers. With the topmost layer, lay out the tomato rings and greens in one bunch, so that later it will be convenient to remove them. Cover the cauldron tightly with a lid and place over medium heat. As soon as you understand that the booglama has already boiled, the fire should be reduced to a minimum and then the dish should be simmer for 1.5 hours.

A lot of tasty liquid is formed in the finished dish, and this is without even adding a drop of water! Pour the chicken booglama into bowls or serve on a shared platter sprinkled with fresh herbs. The meat is the softest, it just melts in your mouth.

Kaurma-pilaf

To cook pilaf in Azerbaijani, forget all the ways you know how to prepare this dish from Asian cuisine.

Namely: we will cook rice separately from meat. We use only ghee butter! In our version, rice is cooked on a thin unleavened flatbread, which is then also served on the table. This cake is called "kazmag".

The common thing is, perhaps, only that at the end of cooking when serving pilaf on the table, we will definitely remember about greens and about sorbet.

Sherbet in Azerbaijan is preferred a little sour, so we cook it with the addition of sour fruits or berries. You can add mint for freshness.

Also, Azerbaijani pilaf is often decorated with fresh pomegranate seeds.
In Azerbaijan, pilaf is cooked with fish, vegetables, eggs, lamb or poultry, as well as fruits.
Today I bring to your attention a pilaf with lamb, which is called "Kaurma-pilaf".

Ingredients:

- Lamb - 750 g
- Onions - 5 pcs.
- Pomegranate - 1 pc.
- Raisins - 1/2 cup
- Melted butter - 100 g
- Flour - 220 g
- Chicken egg - 1 pc.
- Ice water - 1-2 tbsp.
- Salt - to taste
- Turmeric - a pinch
- Pumpkin - 200 g
- Greens

Preparation:

First you need to thoroughly rinse the rice to "clean water".

Put the rice in the water.

Boil the rice until half cooked, put it in a colander and rinse in cold running water ..

Put the rice in a colander cooking.

While the rice is, knead the dough, like for noodles, from flour, eggs and ice water.

Combine flour, egg and water.

Roll the resulting dough thinly, like on noodles. It will be KAZMAG.

Roll out the dough. Color half of the rice with turmeric infusion. To do this, 1 tbsp. mix ghee with 1 tsp. boiling water and add a pinch of turmeric to this mixture.

Mix oil, boiling water and turmeric. Mix half of the deferred rice with this mixture in a separate plate.

In order for the rice to cook completely, the bottom of the cauldron is lined with kazmag, having previously greased with 1/4 part of melted butter on the inside. After that, put half of the rice cooked until half cooked, pour over half of the remaining ghee. Put turmeric-dyed rice on top.

Put butter on top (leaving about 2 tablespoons for browning the meat), smooth the rice thinly, cover tightly and keep on low heat until the rice is cooked.

Mix the rice with turmeric and butter.

Cut the lamb into pieces.

Put the meat in the pan.

Fry in your own fat with the addition of 2 tablespoons. ghee over high heat until golden brown.

Fry the meat.

Dice the onions.

Chop the onion.

Put chopped onion, chopped pumpkin, pomegranate juice, raisins and roasted lamb into a cauldron or a thick-walled saucepan. Pour everything with half a glass of boiling water, salt to taste and simmer over low heat under a lid for 30-45 minutes.

Combine meat, vegetables, pomegranate juice and raisins

Put the boiled rice on a dish, put the separately boiled meat with vegetables and raisins on top.

Sprinkle with pomegranate seeds on top.

KAZMAG is torn to pieces and served with pilaf. We also serve greens, which we have in our house, to the Azerbaijani pilaf: green onions, mint, parsley or cilantro.

Tava Kebab

In the countries of the Caucasus and the Middle East, there is no concept of "fried meat", but there is a stable "kebab".

On the hearing of meat lovers, except for kebab, perhaps there was nothing else like it. It turns out that there are not so few variations in the preparation of kebabs.

On the pages of Persian books, according to Wikipedia, "kebab" means meatballs made from minced meat. The modern "kebab" is a grilled cutlet.

Fragrant fried cutlets baked in an omelet mass with onions, tomatoes, bell peppers and herbs. I like this dish.

What could be tastier than homemade cutlets in an omelet with vegetables?

Let's go make tava kebab!

Ingredients:

- Minced meat - 600 g
- Onions - 2 heads
- Chicken egg - 5-6 pcs.
- Fresh greens - to taste
- Salt - to taste
- A mixture of spicy peppers - to taste Ghee
- butter - 50 g
- Bulgarian pepper (red) - 1/2 pc.

Preparation:

The classic Azerbaijani kebab is made from lamb. If desired, you can replace it with veal and even chicken.

Minced meat should not be too fatty. Dilute it with onions. In this case, you need very little onion. The bulk of the fried onions will go into the omelet. Season the minced meat with salt and spices.

Mix and beat carefully with your hands. To make it easier to beat off the minced meat, we wet our hands in water. We pick up the minced meat in the palm of our hand and throw it with force into the bowl. From well-beaten minced meat, elastic kebabs are obtained.

The molding is similar to meatballs, only the kebab is slightly larger in size. Let's dip our hands into the water. We take part of the minced meat one by one. We roll the minced meat into balls, and then form the meatballs. Preheat a frying pan with ghee. Fry our kebabs in oil first on one side. Note that no kebab flour is used.

Turn over and fry until golden brown on the other.

Whisk chicken eggs in a separate bowl. Add chopped herbs and fried onions. A little salt. Saute the onions in ghee in a separate frying pan.
Take a small frying pan without a handle. Heat slightly. Lubricate with ghee. Put the kebab in the middle. Fill with the egg mixture. Put bell pepper cubes or tomatoes in the intervals between cutlets. We send it to a preheated oven for 15-20 minutes.
The tava kebab is ready!

Yalanchi-dolma

Yalanchi-dolma is a delicious vegetarian dish, also called false dolma. Probably, it is customary to eat such a dish with meat filling, but there is also a lean recipe, which is very satisfying and tasty.

The first time I tried this dish from a friend, she was fasting at that moment and invited me to dinner. To be honest, I didn't immediately realize that there was no meat in the filling, it was very satisfying

Ingredients:

- Salted grape leaves - 15 pcs.
- Rice - 0.5 cups
- Bulgarian pepper - 1/2 pc.
- Bulb onions - 1/2 pc.
- Dried paprika - 1/2 tsp
- Oregano - 1 tsp
- Greens - to taste
- Salt - to taste
- Pepper - to taste
- Vegetable oil - for frying

Preparation:

Let's start the filling. First, heat a frying pan with vegetable oil and fry the chopped onion until soft.

Add oregano and paprika.

Rinse the rice and put it in a pan with the onion, heat for about 3 minutes, stirring constantly, over medium heat.

By the way, long-grain rice is used for this recipe, but I prefer round-grain rice, I like it more in this dish, you can add any one according to your taste.

Then we cut the pepper into small pieces, chop the greens finely and put them in rice, pour in a little water, 0.5 cups is enough. Evaporate, stirring, and remove from heat, the rice should be half cooked.

If the grape leaves are salty, you do not need to salt the filling.

If the grape leaves are very salty, rinse under running water, then put the filling on the matte side of the leaf.

Fold the edges to the center and roll them into tubes.

Put the blanks in a refractory dish or stewpan, pour water to half the dolma, cover and simmer over medium heat for about 25 minutes, or bake in the oven.

Yalanchi-dolma is ready, served hot with yogurt or sour cream.

Ovrishta

Ovrishta is a simple but very tasty recipe for fried chicken with dogwood and onion according to the Azerbaijani recipe.

Ingredients:

- Chicken thighs - 3 pcs.
- Cornel - 200 g
- Onions - 2 pcs.
- Salt - to taste
- Sugar - to taste
- Pepper h.m. - to taste

- Mint - for serving
- Vegetable oil - 1 tbsp.

Preparation:

Peel the onion, wash with chicken and mint under running water, dry. Dogwood can be taken fresh, frozen or dried.

Heat vegetable oil in a frying pan, fry chicken thighs in it on both sides until golden brown - 10-15 minutes on each side. Season with salt and pepper to taste.

Put onion sliced into the same oil.

Fry over low heat for 5 minutesAdd dogwood and a little sugar, simmer over low heat for 5 minutes, crush a couple of berries with a fork, try not to overexpose the rest so that they remain intact.

Return the chicken to the pan, pour in a little water, simmer for 5 minutes maximum. Season the dish with a little salt and pepper.

Place the chicken on a plate, top with the fried dogwood and onion, pour over the sauce. When serving, sprinkle with fresh mint over Ovrishta.

Fried chicken with dogwood and onion is ready.

Piti

Piti is a very tasty and hearty Azerbaijani soup with very little broth.

Piti is a soup that belongs to Azerbaijani cuisine. Of course, now this soup has been interpreted a little with more affordable ingredients that can be bought anywhere and anytime. So, for example, chestnuts began to be replaced with potatoes, lamb or beef - a matter of taste. But it is imperative to add sour plum or cherry plum, mint and chickpeas to the soup.

- Mint - for serving
- Vegetable oil - 1 tbsp.

Preparation:

Peel the onion, wash with chicken and mint under running water, dry. Dogwood can be taken fresh, frozen or dried.

Heat vegetable oil in a frying pan, fry chicken thighs in it on both sides until golden brown - 10-15 minutes on each side. Season with salt and pepper to taste.

Put onion sliced into the same oil.

Fry over low heat for 5 minutesAdd dogwood and a little sugar, simmer over low heat for 5 minutes, crush a couple of berries with a fork, try not to overexpose the rest so that they remain intact.

Return the chicken to the pan, pour in a little water, simmer for 5 minutes maximum. Season the dish with a little salt and pepper.

Place the chicken on a plate, top with the fried dogwood and onion, pour over the sauce. When serving, sprinkle with fresh mint over Ovrishta.

Fried chicken with dogwood and onion is ready.

Piti

Piti is a very tasty and hearty Azerbaijani soup with very little broth.

Piti is a soup that belongs to Azerbaijani cuisine. Of course, now this soup has been interpreted a little with more affordable ingredients that can be bought anywhere and anytime. So, for example, chestnuts began to be replaced with potatoes, lamb or beef - a matter of taste. But it is imperative to add sour plum or cherry plum, mint and chickpeas to the soup.

The soup is cooked in the oven, instead of the lid, lard is used, which is used to cover the pots of soup, during the baking process the lard will brown. Traditionally, piti is served to the table as two separate dishes: in one plate - yushka with lavash, in the other plate - meat, potatoes, chickpeas and onions with tomatoes.

Ingredients:

- Beef - 300 g
- Potatoes - 2 pcs.
- Young onions - 40 g
- Tomatoes - 2 pcs.
- Lard - 60 g
- Water / broth - 250-300 ml
- Plum - 4 pcs.
- Dry mint - 4 leaves
- Garlic - 2 cloves
- Greens - to taste
- Salt, pepper - to taste
- Sumakh - 1/4 tsp.
- Chickpeas - 70 g

Preparation:

Prepare two pots or one large clay pot for the oven.

Chickpeas should be soaked in cool water in advance, you can leave it overnight or for three hours. My chickpeas increase in volume in three hours. Then drain the water.

Soak chickpeas.

Cut the young onions and potatoes into medium sized pieces.

Chop the potatoes and onions.

Put 6-8 slices of beef or lamb in the bottom of each pot. The meat should completely cover the bottom of the mold. When we start filling the pots, turn on the oven and heat it up to 150 degrees.

Place the meat in the pot.

Then spread the potatoes and onions over the meat. You can take an ordinary onion, it should be cut into rings or half rings.

Put onions and potatoes on the meat.

Put a handful of chickpeas, which were soaked in advance, on top. Also, one or two plums should be added to each pot.

Add chickpeas and plums.

Cut the tomato into cubes and add to each mold. Pour in a little water or broth. Add dry mint.

Add tomatoes and mint.

Cover each pan with bacon. Also add sumac, salt and pepper to your taste. In addition, it is worth putting at least a clove of garlic in each mold. Bake piti at 150 degrees for an hour, then lower the temperature to 100 degrees, bake for another hour.

Add pieces of bacon.

Serve the Azerbaijani piti soup to the table straight from the oven.

www.ingramcontent.com/pod-product-compliance
Ingram Content Group UK Ltd.
Pitfield, Milton Keynes, MK11 3LW, UK
UKHW061829190726
13853UKWH00009B/2509